FIFA CLUB WORLD CUP 2025™

CB140608

2

3

4

NATIONALITIES

ALGERIA	CROATIA	ITALY	NORWAY	SPAIN
ANGOLA	DENMARK	IVORY COAST	PALESTINE	SWEDEN
ARGENTINA	ECUADOR	JAPAN	PARAGUAY	SWITZERLAND
ARMENIA	EGYPT	KOREA REPUBLIC	PERU	TOGO
AUSTRIA	ENGLAND	LUXEMBOURG	POLAND	TUNISIA
BELGIUM	FRANCE	MALI	PORTUGAL	TURKEY
BRAZIL	GEORGIA	MEXICO	SAUDI ARABIA	UKRAINE
CANADA	GERMANY	MOROCCO	SENEGAL	UNITED ARAB EMIRATES
CHILE	GREECE	NAMIBIA	SERBIA	UNITED STATES OF AMERICA
CHINA	GUINEA	NETHERLANDS	SLOVENIA	URUGUAY
COLOMBIA	ISRAEL	NEW ZEALAND	SOUTH AFRICA	VENEZUELA

Contents and data last updated: 3 February 2025

STADIUMS

Find out more at
FIFA.com

Mercedes-Benz Stadium
Location: Atlanta, GA
Capacity: 75,000
Opened: 2017

MetLife Stadium
Location: New York New Jersey
Capacity: 82,500
Opened: 2010

Bank of America Stadium
Location: Charlotte, NC.
Capacity: 75,000
Opened: 1996

Camping World Stadium
Location: Orlando, FL
Capacity: 65,000
Opened: 1936

TQL Stadium
Location: Cincinnati, OH
Capacity: 26,000
Opened: 2021

Inter&Co Stadium
Location: Orlando, FL
Capacity: 25,000
Opened: 2017

Rose Bowl Stadium
Location: Los Angeles, CA
Capacity: 88,500
Opened: 1922

Lincoln Financial Field
Location: Philadelphia, PA
Capacity: 69,000
Opened: 2003

Hard Rock Stadium
Location: Miami, FL
Capacity: 65,000
Opened: 1987

Lumen Field
Location: Seattle, WA
Capacity: 69,000
Opened: 2002

GEODIS Park
Location: Nashville, TN
Capacity: 30,000
Opened: 2022

Audi Field
Location: Washington, D.C.
Capacity: 20,000
Opened: 2018

Data source: FIFA.com

NEW YORK NEW JERSEY
PHILADELPHIA
WASHINGTON, D.C.
CINCINNATI
NASHVILLE
CHARLOTTE
ATLANTA
ORLANDO
MIAMI

CLUB WORLD CUP 25

FIFA

FIFA CLUB WORLD CUP 2025™

MATCH SCHEDULE

GROUP STAGE

	14 JUNE Saturday	15 JUNE Sunday	16 JUNE Monday	17 JUNE Tuesday	18 JUNE Wednesday	19 JUNE Thursday	20 JUNE Friday	21 JUNE Saturday	22 JUNE Sunday	23 JUNE Monday	24 JUNE Tuesday	25 JUNE Wednesday	26 JUNE Thursday
ATLANTA Mercedes-Benz Stadium			6 15:00 CHE v LEO			18 15:00 MIA v POR			32 21:00 MCI v AIN				
CHARLOTTE Bank of America Stadium									30 15:00 RMA v PAC		38 15:00 SLB v BAY		
CINCINNATI TQL Stadium		2 12:00 BAY v AKL			15 18:00 PAC v SAL			25 12:00 MSU v BVB				41 15:00 BVB v UHD	
LOS ANGELES Rose Bowl Stadium *PT (ET - 3)		3 12:00 PSG v ATM		12 18:00 CFM v INT		20 18:00 PSG v BOT		28 18:00 RIV v CFM		34 12:00 ATM v BOT		44 18:00 URD v CFM	
MIAMI Hard Rock Stadium	1 20:00 AHL v MIA		7 18:00 BOC v SLB		14 15:00 RMA v HIL		24 21:00 BAY v BOC			35 21:00 MIA v PAL		42 15:00 MSU v FLU	
NASHVILLE GEODIS Park *CT (ET - 1)							23 17:00 LEO v EST				37 14:00 AKL v BOC		47 20:00 HIL v PAC
NEW YORK NEW JERSEY MetLife Stadium		4 18:00 PAL v POR		9 12:00 FLU v BVB		17 12:00 PAL v AHL		27 18:00 FLU v UHD		36 21:00 POR v AHL			
ORLANDO Camping World Stadium											39 21:00 LEO v FLA		45 15:00 JUV v MCI
ORLANDO Inter&Co Stadium				11 18:00 UHD v MSU			21 12:00 SLB v AKL						
PHILADELPHIA Lincoln Financial Field			8 21:00 FLA v EST		13 12:00 MCI v WAC		22 14:00 FLA v CHE		29 12:00 JUV v WAC		40 21:00 EST v CHE		48 21:00 SAL v RMA
SEATTLE Lumen Field *PT (ET - 3)		5 19:00 BOT v SEA		10 12:00 RIV v URD		19 15:00 SEA v ATM		26 12:00 INT v URD		33 12:00 SEA v PSG		43 18:00 INT v RIV	
WASHINGTON, D.C. Audi Field					16 21:00 AIN v JUV				31 18:00 SAL v HIL				46 15:00 WAC v AIN

All kick-off times are local time. Kick-off times are subject to change.
*All cities are ET except Nashville CT (ET - 1), Seattle and Los Angeles PT (ET - 3)

GROUP A	GROUP B	GROUP C	GROUP D	GROUP E
SE Palmeiras (PAL)	Paris Saint-Germain (PSG)	FC Bayern Munchen (BAY)	CR Flamengo (FLA)	CA River Plate (RIV)
FC Porto (POR)	Atlético de Madrid (ATM)	Auckland City FC (AKL)	Espérance Sportive de Tunisie (EST)	Urawa Red Diamonds (URD)
Al Ahly FC (AHL)	Botafogo (BOT)	CA Boca Juniors (BOC)	Chelsea FC (CHE)	CF Monterrey (CFM)
Inter Miami CF (MIA)	Seattle Sounders FC (SEA)	SL Benfica (SLB)	Club León (LEO)	FC Internazionale Milano (INT)

	ROUND OF 16						QUARTER FINALS				SEMI FINALS					FINAL
	27 JUNE Friday	**28 JUNE** Saturday	**29 JUNE** Sunday	**30 JUNE** Monday	**1 JULY** Tuesday	**2 JULY** Wednesday	**3 JULY** Thursday	**4 JULY** Friday	**5 JULY** Saturday	**6 JULY** Sunday	**7 JULY** Monday	**8 JULY** Tuesday	**9 JULY** Wednesday	**10 JULY** Thursday	**11 JULY** Friday	**12 JULY** Saturday	**13 JULY** Sunday

27 June, Friday	REST DAY
28 June, Saturday	50 16:00 1C v 2D; 49 12:00 1A v 2B
29 June, Sunday	51 12:00 1B v 2A; 52 16:00 1D v 2C
30 June, Monday	53 15:00 1E v 2F; 54 21:00 1G v 2H
1 July, Tuesday	56 21:00 1F v 2E; 55 15:00 1H v 2G
2 July, Wednesday – 3 July, Thursday	REST DAYS
4 July, Friday	57 15:00 W53 v W54; 58 21:00 W49 v W50
5 July, Saturday	59 12:00 W51 v W52; 60 16:00 W55 v W56
6 July, Sunday – 7 July, Monday	REST DAYS
8 July, Tuesday	61 15:00 W57 v W58
9 July, Wednesday	62 15:00 W59 v W60
10 July, Thursday – 12 July, Saturday	REST DAYS
13 July, Sunday	63 FINAL 15:00

GROUP F
Fluminense FC (FLU)
Borussia Dortmund (BVB)
Ulsan HD (UHD)
Mamelodi Sundowns FC (MSU)

GROUP G
Manchester City (MCI)
Wydad AC (WAC)
Al Ain FC (AIN)
Juventus FC (JUV)

GROUP H
Real Madrid C. F. (RMA)
Al Hilal (HIL)
CF Pachuca (PAC)
FC Salzburg (SAL)

© FIFA

São Paulo (Brazil)

SE PALMEIRAS

5	6 WEVERTON	7 JOAQUÍN PIQUEREZ
8 MURILO	9 GUSTAVO GÓMEZ	10 MARCOS ROCHA
11 RICHARD RÍOS	12 ANÍBAL MORENO	13 MAURÍCIO

14
RAPHAEL VEIGA

15
FACUNDO TORRES

16
The Emblem

For the clubs.
A new era of growth

17
PAULINHO

18
ESTÊVÃO

19
The Chosen One

For the players.
A new era of greatness

20
JOSÉ MANUEL LÓPEZ

21
FELIPE ANDERSON

22
The Crowd Hero

For the fans.
A new era of pride

GROUP A

PALMEIRAS FCP MIAMI

FC PORTO

Porto (Portugal)

23

24
DIOGO COSTA

25
NEHUEN PÉREZ

26
FRANCISCO MOURA

27
MARTIM FERNANDES

28
JOÃO MÁRIO

29
ZÉ PEDRO

30
OTAVIO

31
ALAN VARELA

32 GONÇALO BORGES	33 STEPHEN EUSTÁQUIO
35 FÁBIO VIEIRA	36 SAMU AGHEHOWA
38 PEPÊ	39 DANNY NAMASO

GROUP A

34 The Emblem

For the clubs.
A new era of growth

37 The Chosen One

For the players.
A new era of greatness

40 The Crowd Hero

For the fans.
A new era of pride

AL AHLY FC

Cairo (Egypt)

41	42 MOHAMED ELSHENAWY	43 ALI MAÂLOUL
44 MOHAMED HANY	45 YASSER IBRAHIM	46 RAMI RABIA
47 OMAR KAMAL	48 EMAM ASHOUR	49 MARAWAN ATTIA

50
AFSHA

51
AMR EL SOLIA

52
The Emblem

For the clubs.
A new era of growth

53
ACHRAF BENCHARKI

54
WESSAM ABOU ALI

55
The Chosen One

For the players.
A new era of greatness

56
HUSSEIN ELSHAHAT

57
TAHER MOHAMED

58
The Crowd Hero

For the fans.
A new era of pride

GROUP A

PALMEIRAS · FCP · MIAMI

INTER MIAMI CF

Miami (USA)

7-10-1997 DRAKE CALLENDER

3-2-2004 TOMÁS AVILÉS

21-3-1989 JORDI ALBA

11-1-2000 MARCELO WEIGANDT

21-1-1998 DAVID MARTÍNEZ

28-4-2004 NOAH ALLEN

2-3-2005 BENJAMIN CREMASCHI

8-2-2004 DAVID RUÍZ

18-1-2003 FEDERICO REDONDO

16-12-1993 JULIAN GRESSEL

16-7-1988 SERGIO BUSQUETS

24-6-1987 LIONEL MESSI

24-1-1987 LUIS SUÁREZ

21-10-1994 ROBERT TAYLOR

GROUP A

MIAMI

59

The Emblem

For the clubs.
A new era of growth

60

The Chosen One

For the players.
A new era of greatness

61

The Crowd Hero

For the fans.
A new era of pride

Get your tickets at
FIFA.com/tickets

Watch every game. Free. On DAZN.com

EXCLUSIVE GLOBAL BROADCASTER

DAZN

FIFA CLUB WORLD CUP 2025 PARTNERS

ULTRA

BANK OF AMERICA

Coca-Cola

Hisense

PARIS SAINT-GERMAIN

Paris (France)

62	63 GIANLUIGI DONNARUMMA	64 ACHRAF HAKIMI
65 NUNO MENDES	66 MARQUINHOS	67 LUCAS BERALDO
68 LUCAS HERNÁNDEZ	69 WARREN ZAÏRE-EMERY	70 JOÃO NEVES

71
VITINHA

72
LEE KANG-IN

73
The Emblem

For the clubs.
A new era of growth

74
FABIÁN RUIZ

75
BRADLEY BARCOLA

76
The Chosen One

For the players.
A new era of greatness

77
OUSMANE DEMBÉLÉ

78
GONÇALO RAMOS

79
The Crowd Hero

For the fans.
A new era of pride

GROUP B

PARIS SEATTLE

ATLÉTICO DE MADRID

Madrid (Spain)

80	81 JAN OBLAK	82 ROBIN LE NORMAND
83 NAHUEL MOLINA	84 JOSÉ MARÍA GIMÉNEZ	85 AXEL WITSEL
86 CONOR GALLAGHER	87 RODRIGO DE PAUL	88 MARCOS LLORENTE

89
KOKE

90
JULIÁN ALVAREZ

91
The Emblem
For the clubs.
A new era of growth

92
SAMUEL LINO

93
ANTOINE GRIEZMANN

94
The Chosen One
For the players.
A new era of greatness

95
ALEXANDER SØRLOTH

96
ÁNGEL CORREA

97
The Crowd Hero
For the fans.
A new era of pride

GROUP B

PARIS

SEATTLE

BOTAFOGO

Rio de Janeiro (Brazil)

98

99
JOHN VICTOR

100
VITINHO

101
ALEXANDER BARBOZA

102
BASTOS

103
JAIR

104
MATEO PONTE

105
ALEX TELLES

106
CUIABANO

107

JEFFERSON SAVARINO

108

MARLON FREITAS

110

GREGORE

111

IGOR JESUS

113

ARTUR

114

MATHEUS MARTINS

GROUP B

PARIS

SEATTLE

109

The Emblem

For the clubs.
A new era of growth

112

The Chosen One

For the players.
A new era of greatness

115

The Crowd Hero

For the fans.
A new era of pride

SEATTLE SOUNDERS FC

Seattle (USA)

20-4-1986 STEFAN FREI

23-6-1997 NOUHOU

28-7-1996 ÁLEX ROLDÁN

30-6-1992 YEIMAR GÓMEZ

24-9-1998 JACKSON RAGEN

5-5-2003 DANNY LEYVA

3-6-1995 CRISTIAN ROLDÁN

5-8-2005 OBED VARGAS

7-7-1994 ALBERT RUSNÁK

5-2-1995 PAUL ARRIOLA

7-2-2001 PEDRO DE LA VEGA

26-10-1994 JORDAN MORRIS

24-12-2000 JESÚS FERREIRA

9-1-1999 PAUL ROTHROCK

116

The Emblem

For the clubs.
A new era of growth

117

The Chosen One

For the players.
A new era of greatness

118

The Crowd Hero

For the fans.
A new era of pride

GROUP B

PARIS

SEATTLE

FIFA CLUB WORLD CUP 2025™

PANINI | FIFA COLLECT

PANINI TAKES YOU TO FIFA WORLD CUP 26™ & FIFA CLUB WORLD CUP 2025™

Join FIFA Collect, where your passion meets the chance to secure tickets for these legendary tournaments.

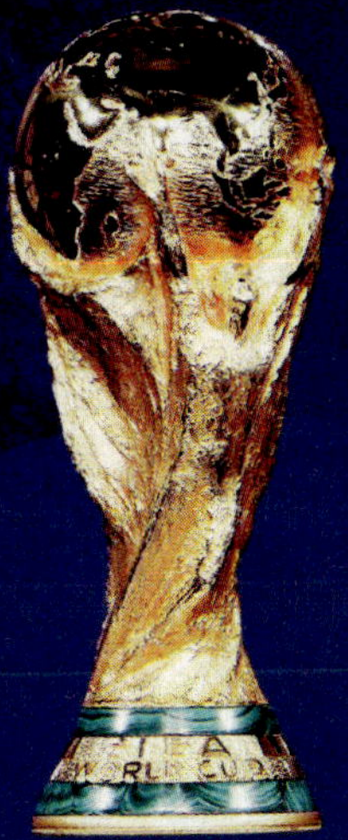

GET YOUR FREE PACK FOR A CHANCE AT FOOTBALL'S BIGGEST STAGES

1. **Scan the QR code** with your smartphone

2. **Sign up** on FIFA Collect

3. **Claim your** Free Pack

FIFA COLLECT is a platform that allows users to purchase, collect, and showcase collectibles in the form of non-fungible tokens (NFTs) featuring content licensed by the Fédération Internationale de Football Association (FIFA), clubs, and federations. Terms of Service apply – see https://collect.fifa.com/terms-of-service.

FC BAYERN MÜNCHEN

Munich (Germany)

119	120 MANUEL NEUER	121 ALPHONSO DAVIES
122 DAYOT UPAMECANO	123 MINJAE KIM	124 RAPHAËL GUERREIRO
125 JAMAL MUSIALA	126 JOSHUA KIMMICH	127 ALEKSANDAR PAVLOVIĆ

128
HARRY KANE

129
MICHAEL OLISE

131
LEROY SANÉ

132
SERGE GNABRY

134
THOMAS MÜLLER

135
KINGSLEY COMAN

130
The Emblem

For the clubs.
A new era of growth

133
The Chosen One

For the players.
A new era of greatness

136
The Crowd Hero

For the fans.
A new era of pride

GROUP C

AUCKLAND CITY FC

Auckland (New Zealand)

137	138 CONOR TRACEY	139 NATHAN LOBO
140 ALFIE ROGERS	141 ADAM MITCHELL	142 MICHAEL DEN HEIJER
143 JORDAN VALE	144 CHRISTIAN GRAY	145 MARIO ILICH

146
GERARD GARRIGA

147
DYLAN MANICKUM

148
The Emblem

For the clubs.
A new era of growth

149
TONG ZHOU

150
JOSEPH LEE

151
The Chosen One

For the players.
A new era of greatness

152
RYAN DE VRIES

153
ANGUS KILKOLLY

154
The Crowd Hero

For the fans.
A new era of pride

GROUP C

CLUB ATLÉTICO BOCA JUNIORS

Buenos Aires (Argentina)

155	156 AGUSTÍN MARCHESÍN	157 AYRTON COSTA
158 MARCELO SARACCHI	159 LUIS ADVÍNCULA	160 MARCOS ROJO
161 RODRIGO BATTAGLIA	162 TOMÁS BELMONTE	163 ANDER HERRERA

164
CARLOS PALACIOS

165
EXEQUIEL ZEBALLOS

166
The Emblem

For the clubs.
A new era of growth

167
ALAN VELASCO

168
MIGUEL MERENTIEL

169
The Chosen One

For the players.
A new era of greatness

170
EDINSON CAVANI

171
MILTON GIMÉNEZ

172
The Crowd Hero

For the fans.
A new era of pride

GROUP C

SL BENFICA

Lisbon (Portugal)

173	174 ANATOLIY TRUBIN	175 ANTÓNIO SILVA
176 TOMÁS ARAÚJO	177 ALEXANDER BAH	178 NICOLÁS OTAMENDI
179 ÁLVARO CARRERAS	180 ORKUN KÖKCÜ	181 FREDRIK AURSNES

182
FLORENTINO

183
LEANDRO BARREIRO

184
The Emblem

For the clubs.
A new era of growth

185
VANGELIS PAVLIDIS

186
KEREM AKTÜRKOĞLU

187
The Chosen One

For the players.
A new era of greatness

188
ÁNGEL DI MARÍA

189
ZEKI AMDOUNI

190
The Crowd Hero

For the fans.
A new era of pride

GROUP C

CR FLAMENGO

Rio de Janeiro (Brazil)

191	192 AGUSTÍN ROSSI	193 LÉO ORTIZ
194 LÉO PEREIRA	195 ALEX SANDRO	196 WESLEY
197 DANILO	198 NICOLÁS DE LA CRUZ	199 GIORGIAN DE ARRASCAETA

200

GERSON

201

ERICK PULGAR

202

The Emblem

For the clubs.
A new era of growth

203

MICHAEL

204

PEDRO

205

The Chosen One

For the players.
A new era of greatness

206

EVERTON

207

BRUNO HENRIQUE

208

The Crowd Hero

For the fans.
A new era of pride

GROUP D

ESPÉRANCE SPORTIVE DE TUNIS

Tunis (Tunisia)

209	210 AMANALLAH MEMMICHE	211 YASSINE MERIAH
212 MOHAMED AMINE BEN HAMIDA	213 RAED BOUCHNIBA	214 MOHAMED AMINE TOUGAI
215 HAMZA JELASSI	216 HOUSSEM TKA	217 LARRY AZOUNI

218
ELIAS MOKWANA

219
ROGER AHOLOU

220
The Emblem

For the clubs.
A new era of growth

221
YOUCEF BELAÏLI

222
YAN SASSE

223
The Chosen One

For the players.
A new era of greatness

224
RODRIGO RODRIGUES

225
ZINEDINE KADA

226
The Crowd Hero

For the fans.
A new era of pride

GROUP D

CHELSEA FC

London (England)

227	228 ROBERT SÁNCHEZ	229 LEVI COLWILL
230 MALO GUSTO	231 MARC CUCURELLA	232 WESLEY FOFANA
233 TOSIN ADARABIOYO	234 ENZO FERNÁNDEZ	235 MOISÉS CAICEDO

236
COLE PALMER

237
CHRISTOPHER NKUNKU

238
The Emblem
For the clubs.
A new era of growth

239
NICOLAS JACKSON

240
PEDRO NETO

241
The Chosen One
For the players.
A new era of greatness

242
JADON SANCHO

243
NONI MADUEKE

244
The Crowd Hero
For the fans.
A new era of pride

GROUP D

My DREAM TEAM

Use your doubles here! Create your 'Dream Team' with your best starting 11!

Nutze hier deine doppelten Sticker! Stelle dein „Dream Team" mit den besten Spielern zusammen! · Colle tes doubles ici ! Crée ta "Dream Team" en choisissant le onze de départ de tes rêves ! · Incolla qui le tue figurine doppie! Crea il tuo "Dream Team" schierando l'undici iniziale che preferisci! · Gebruik hier je dubbele! Stel je 'Dreamteam' samen met je beste 11 in de basis! · ¡Pega aquí tus cromos dobles! ¡ Crea tu propio 'Dream Team' eligiendo a tus once jugadores favoritos. ·

Utiliza aqui os teus duplos! Cria a tua "equipa de sonho" com o teu melhor 11 inicial! · Çiftlerini burada kullan! "Rüya Takımını" kur ve ilk 11'ini seç! · Tu możesz wykorzystać dublety swoich naklejek! Stwórz swą 'Drużynę Marzeń' z najlepszą wyjściową jedenastką. · Используйте свои повторные наклейки здесь!Создайте свою "Команду мечты" из 11 своих лучших игроков стартового состава!"

CLUB LEÓN

León (Mexico)

245	246 ALFONSO BLANCO	247 STIVEN BARREIRO
248 SALVADOR REYES	249 IVÁN MORENO	250 DAVID RAMÍREZ
251 ADONIS FRÍAS	252 RODRIGO ECHEVERRÍA	253 ÁNGEL ESTRADA

254
SEBASTIÁN SANTOS

255
ANDRÉS GUARDADO

256
The Emblem

For the clubs.
A new era of growth

257
JHONDER CÁDIZ

258
JAMES RODRÍGUEZ

259
The Chosen One

For the players.
A new era of greatness

260
STIVEN MENDOZA

261
EDGAR GUERRA

262
The Crowd Hero

For the fans.
A new era of pride

GROUP D

CA RIVER PLATE

Buenos Aires (Argentina)

263	264 FRANCO ARMANI	265 FABRICIO BUSTOS
266 PAULO DÍAZ	267 LUCAS MARTÍNEZ QUARTA	268 GONZALO MONTIEL
269 MARCOS ACUÑA	270 ENZO PÉREZ	271 FRANCO MASTANTUONO

272
SANTIAGO SIMÓN

273
NACHO FERNÁNDEZ

274
The Emblem

For the clubs.
A new era of growth

275
RODRIGO ALIENDRO

276
SEBASTIÁN DRIUSSI

277
The Chosen One

For the players.
A new era of greatness

278
FACUNDO COLIDIO

279
MIGUEL BORJA

280
The Crowd Hero

For the fans.
A new era of pride

GROUP E

URAWA RED DIAMONDS

Saitama (Japan)

281

282
SHUSAKU NISHIKAWA

283
MARIUS HØIBRÅTEN

284
TAKUYA OGIWARA

285
TAISHI MATSUMOTO

286
SAMUEL GUSTAFSON

287
MATHEUS SAVIO

288
RYOMA WATANABE

289
KAITO YASUI

290
TAKAHIRO SEKINE

291
SHOYA NAKAJIMA

292
The Emblem

For the clubs.
A new era of growth

293
TAKURO KANEKO

294
GENKI HARAGUCHI

295
The Chosen One

For the players.
A new era of greatness

296
YUSUKE MATSUO

297
THIAGO SANTANA

298
The Crowd Hero

For the fans.
A new era of pride

GROUP E

CF MONTERREY

Monterrey (Mexico)

299

300
ESTEBAN ANDRADA

301
VÍCTOR GUZMÁN

302
GERARDO ARTEAGA

303
STEFAN MEDINA

304
SERGIO RAMOS

305
HÉCTOR MORENO

306
NELSON DEOSSA

307
SERGIO CANALES

308
JORGE RODRÍGUEZ

309
ÓLIVER TORRES

310
The Emblem

For the clubs.
A new era of growth

311
GERMÁN BERTERAME

312
LUCAS OCAMPOS

313
The Chosen One

For the players.
A new era of greatness

314
JORDI CORTIZO

315
JESÚS MANUEL CORONA

316
The Crowd Hero

For the fans.
A new era of pride

GROUP E

FC INTERNAZIONALE MILANO

Milan (Italy)

317	318 YANN SOMMER	319 ALESSANDRO BASTONI
320 FEDERICO DIMARCO	321 BENJAMIN PAVARD	322 DENZEL DUMFRIES
323 FRANCESCO ACERBI	324 MATTEO DARMIAN	325 STEFAN DE VRIJ

326
NICOLÒ BARELLA

327
HAKAN ÇALHANOĞLU

328
The Emblem

For the clubs.
A new era of growth

329
HENRIKH MKHITARYAN

330
PIOTR ZIELIŃSKI

331
The Chosen One

For the players.
A new era of greatness

332
LAUTARO MARTÍNEZ

333
MARCUS THURAM

334
The Crowd Hero

For the fans.
A new era of pride

GROUP E

FLUMINENSE FC

Rio de Janeiro (Brazil)

335	336 FÁBIO	337 THIAGO SILVA
338 MANOEL	339 SAMUEL XAVIER	340 THIAGO SANTOS
341 MARTINELLI	342 LIMA	343 GANSO

344

HÉRCULES

345

AGUSTÍN CANOBBIO

346

The Emblem

For the clubs.
A new era of growth

347

GERMÁN CANO

348

KENO

349

The Chosen One

For the players.
A new era of greatness

350

RIQUELME FELIPE

351

JHON ARIAS

352

The Crowd Hero

For the fans.
A new era of pride

GROUP F

BORUSSIA DORTMUND

Dortmund (Germany)

353	354 GREGOR KOBEL	355 NICO SCHLOTTERBECK
356 JULIAN RYERSON	357 NIKLAS SÜLE	358 RAMY BENSEBAINI
359 WALDEMAR ANTON	360 JULIAN BRANDT	361 MARCEL SABITZER

362
EMRE CAN

363
PASCAL GROß

364
The Emblem

For the clubs.
A new era of growth

365
SERHOU GUIRASSY

366
KARIM ADEYEMI

367
The Chosen One

For the players.
A new era of greatness

368
JULIEN DURANVILLE

369
JAMIE GITTENS

370
The Crowd Hero

For the fans.
A new era of pride

GROUP F

ULSAN HD FC

Ulsan (Korea Republic)

371	372 HYEON-WOO JO	373 SEOK-HO HWANG
374 SANG-WOO KANG	375 YOUNG-GWON KIM	376 JIN-HYUN LEE
377 DARIJAN BOJANIĆ	378 HUI-GYUN LEE	379 SEUNG-BEOM KO

380
GYU-SUNG LEE

381
WOO-YOUNG JUNG

383
GUSTAV LUDWIGSON

384
WON-SANG UM

386
YAGO CARIELLO

387
CHUNG-YONG LEE

GROUP F

382
The Emblem

For the clubs.
A new era of growth

385
The Chosen One

For the players.
A new era of greatness

388
The Crowd Hero

For the fans.
A new era of pride

MAMELODI SUNDOWNS FC

Pretoria (South Africa)

389	390 RONWEN WILLIAMS	391 AUBREY MODIBA
392 KHULISO MUDAU	393 THAPELO MORENA	394 GRANT KEKANA
395 MOSA LEBUSA	396 MALIBONGWE KHOZA	397 TEBOHO MOKOENA

398
MARCELO ALLENDE

399
THEMBA ZWANE

400
The Emblem

For the clubs.
A new era of growth

401
PETER SHALULILE

402
LUCAS RIBEIRO

403
The Chosen One

For the players.
A new era of greatness

404
IQRAAM RAYNERS

405
TASHREEQ MATTHEWS

406
The Crowd Hero

For the fans.
A new era of pride

GROUP F

MANCHESTER CITY

Manchester (England)

407	408 EDERSON	409 RÚBEN DIAS
410 JOŠKO GVARDIOL	411 MANUEL AKANJI	412 JOHN STONES
413 RODRI	414 BERNARDO SILVA	415 KEVIN DE BRUYNE

FIFA CLUB WORLD CUP 2025™

416
İLKAY GÜNDOĞAN

417
MATEO KOVAČIĆ

418
The Emblem

For the clubs.
A new era of growth

419
OMAR MARMOUSH

420
ERLING HAALAND

421
The Chosen One

For the players.
A new era of greatness

422
PHIL FODEN

423
JÉRÉMY DOKU

424
The Crowd Hero

For the fans.
A new era of pride

GROUP G

WYDAD AC

Casablanca (Morocco)

425

426
YOUSSEF EL MOTIE

427
JAMAL HARKASS

428
MOHAMED MOUFID

429
ABDELMOUNAIM BOUTOUIL

430
AYOUB BOUCHETA

431
SAIFEDDINE BOUHRA

432
HAMZA SAKHI

433
ARTHUR WENDERROSCKY

434
MEHDI MOUBARIK

435
OUSSAMA ZEMRAOUI

436
The Emblem

For the clubs.
A new era of growth

437
ISMAIL MOUTARAJI

438
PEDRINHO

439
The Chosen One

For the players.
A new era of greatness

440
CASSIUS MAILULA

441
MOHAMED RAYHI

442
The Crowd Hero

For the fans.
A new era of pride

GROUP G

AL AIN FC

Al Ain (United Arab Emirates)

443

444
KHALID EISA

445
KOUAME AUTONNE

446
KHALID AL HASHEMI

447
ERIK MENEZES

448
SOLOMON SOSU

449
ABDOUL TRAORE

450
YAHIA NADER

451
MOHAMED ABBAS

452 KAKU	453 YONG-WOO PARK
455 MATÍAS PALACIOS	456 MATÍAS SEGOVIA
458 MATEO SANABRIA	459 SOUFIANE RAHIMI

454
The Emblem

For the clubs.
A new era of growth

457
The Chosen One

For the players.
A new era of greatness

460
The Crowd Hero

For the fans.
A new era of pride

GROUP G

JUVENTUS FC

Turin (Italy)

461

462
MICHELE DI GREGORIO

463
BREMER

464
ANDREA CAMBIASO

465
FEDERICO GATTI

466
WESTON McKENNIE

467
TEUN KOOPMEINERS

468
KHÉPHREN THURAM

469
MANUEL LOCATELLI

470

DOUGLAS LUIZ

471

TIMOTHY WEAH

472

The Emblem

For the clubs.
A new era of growth

473

NICO GONZÁLEZ

474

DUŠAN VLAHOVIĆ

475

The Chosen One

For the players.
A new era of greatness

476

KENAN YILDIZ

477

FRANCISCO CONCEIÇÃO

478

The Crowd Hero

For the fans.
A new era of pride

GROUP G

REAL MADRID C.F.

Madrid (Spain)

479	480 THIBAUT COURTOIS	481 ÉDER MILITÃO
482 ANTONIO RÜDIGER	483 DANIEL CARVAJAL	484 JUDE BELLINGHAM
485 FEDERICO VALVERDE	486 AURÉLIEN TCHOUAMÉNI	487 LUKA MODRIĆ

488
EDUARDO CAMAVINGA

489
ARDA GÜLER

490
The Emblem

For the clubs.
A new era of growth

491
VINICIUS JUNIOR

492
KYLIAN MBAPPÉ

493
The Chosen One

For the players.
A new era of greatness

494
ENDRICK

495
RODRYGO

496
The Crowd Hero

For the fans.
A new era of pride

GROUP H

AL HILAL

Riyadh (Saudi Arabia)

497	498 YASSINE BOUNOU	499 JOÃO CANCELO
500 RENAN LODI	501 KALIDOU KOULIBALY	502 ALI AL-BULAIHI
503 MOHAMED KANNO	504 RÚBEN NEVES	505 SERGEJ MILINKOVIĆ-SAVIĆ

506

NASSER AL-DAWSARI

507

KAIO CÉSAR

508

The Emblem

For the clubs.
A new era of growth

509

ALEKSANDAR MITROVIĆ

510

MALCOM

511

The Chosen One

For the players.
A new era of greatness

512

MARCOS LEONARDO

513

SALEM AL-DAWSARI

514

The Crowd Hero

For the fans.
A new era of pride

GROUP H

CF PACHUCA

Pachuca (Mexico)

515

516
CARLOS MORENO

517
BRYAN GONZÁLEZ

518
SERGIO BARRETO

519
LUIS RODRÍGUEZ

520
GUSTAVO CABRAL

521
CARLOS SÁNCHEZ

522
ANDRÉS MICOLTA

523
ALÁN BAUTISTA

524
PEDRO PEDRAZA

525
ELÍAS MONTIEL

526
The Emblem

For the clubs.
A new era of growth

527
ARTURO GONZÁLEZ

528
OUSSAMA IDRISSI

529
The Chosen One

For the players.
A new era of greatness

530
SALOMÓN RONDÓN

531
OWEN GONZÁLEZ

532
The Crowd Hero

For the fans.
A new era of pride

GROUP H

FC SALZBURG

Salzburg (Austria)

533	534 ALEXANDER SCHLAGER	535 HENDRY BLANK
536 SAMSON BAIDOO	537 JOANE GADOU	538 NICOLÁS CAPALDO
539 MAURITS KJÆRGAARD	540 TAKUMU KAWAMURA	541 MADS BIDSTRUP

542
BOBBY CLARK

543
OSCAR GLOUKH

544
The Emblem

For the clubs.
A new era of growth

545
KARIM KONATÉ

546
NENE DORGELES

547
The Chosen One

For the players.
A new era of greatness

548
ADAM DAGHIM

549
YORBE VERTESSEN

550
The Crowd Hero

For the fans.
A new era of pride

GROUP H

GET THE
PANINI COLLECTORS APP

PANINI

SCAN ME

ENJOY THE FUN!

MANAGE your album checklist

SWAP your stickers

COMPLETE your collection

AVAILABLE IN THE MAIN APP STORES

MYPANINI

CREATE YOUR OWN PERSONALISED STICKER WITH THE APP MYPANINI™ !

UPLOAD OR TAKE A PICTURE, PERSONALISE IT AND GET YOUR OWN STICKER!

MYPANINI

www.mypanini.com

The images are for illustration purposes only and may not be an exact representation of the product